ENVIRONMENTAL
ISSUES

BookLife
PUBLISHING

By Emilie Dufresne

BookLife
PUBLISHING

©2019
BookLife Publishing Ltd.
King's Lynn
Norfolk, PE30 4LS

ISBN: 978-1-78637-601-5

Written by:
Emilie Dufresne

Edited by:
Kirsty Holmes

Designed by:
Amy Li

CONTENTS

Words that look like **this** can be found in the glossary on page 24.

WHAT ARE FOSSIL FUELS?

Fossil fuels are types of fuel that have formed over millions of years. They are formed from broken-down plants and animals.

LOTS OF THE FOSSIL FUELS WE USE TODAY WERE FORMED IN THE CARBONIFEROUS (SAY: CAR-BON-IF-ERR-US) PERIOD. THAT'S BEFORE THE DINOSAURS EXISTED!

POWER PLANT BURNING COAL

Fossil fuels are burned to create power. They are non-renewable, which means that once they have been used, they cannot be used again.

TYPES OF FOSSIL FUELS

There are three types of fossil fuels: oil, coal, and natural gas.

OIL

Oil is formed under the sea. It is formed in pockets inside layers of **sediment** that, over the years, turned into rock.

POCKET OF OIL

COAL

Coal is formed of **decomposed** plants and trees that are put under lots of **pressure** by layers of rock forming on top of them. This squeezes the water out of the decomposing material and eventually forms coal.

NATURAL GAS BOTTLES

NATURAL GAS

Natural gas also formed as animals and plants decomposed. The pressure and temperature rose very high. In some cases the temperature rose so much that some fossil fuels **evaporated**, making gas.

7

USES OF FOSSIL FUELS

Fossil fuels are used for lots of different things. One of their main uses is to make energy. They are often burned to produce heat and power. They are used in cars, planes, and central heating.

FOSSIL FUELS CAN ALSO BE USED TO MAKE ELECTRICITY.

From plastic bottles to crayons, the **by-products** of fossil fuels are used for lots of everyday objects. Some other examples include medicine, make-up, and candles.

EFFECTS OF FOSSIL FUELS

Fossil fuels might be used all around the world for lots of different things, but they aren't good for our **environment**. Finding, moving and burning fossil fuels harms our environment, and can make the air **polluted**.

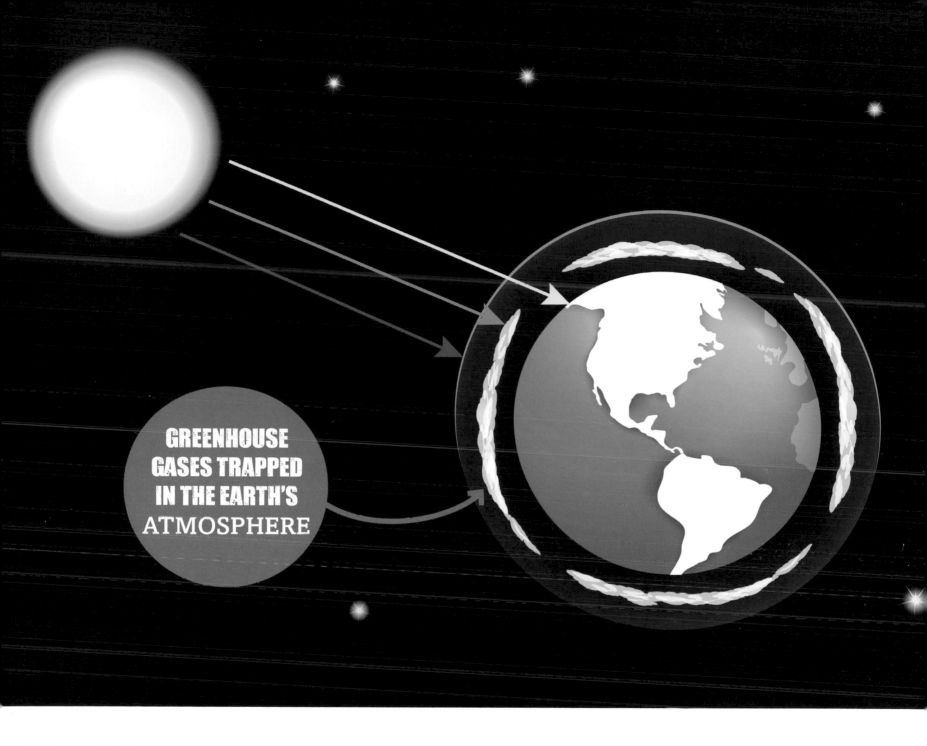

GREENHOUSE
GASES TRAPPED
IN THE EARTH'S
ATMOSPHERE

The air becomes polluted because harmful gases are released when fossil fuels are burned. These are called greenhouse gases. They get trapped in the Earth's atmosphere and make it warmer. Greenhouse gases help to cause **global warming**.

Finding and moving fossil fuels is also bad for the environment. Because fossil fuels are underground, it can be hard to get to them. Mining and fracking are two ways we get to fossil fuels.

BOTH HARM THE ENVIRONMENT IN LOTS OF DIFFERENT WAYS.

FRACKING OIL FIELD, USA

FRACKING CAN MAKE SOME WATER UNSAFE FOR HUMANS TO DRINK.

Mining takes up the space where lots of animals and plants would live. It can also affect how much drinking water we can get from the ground. Fracking releases dangerous gases, such as methanc, into the atmosphere.

FINDING FOSSIL FUELS

THE FOSSIL FUELS ARE PUMPED TO THE SHORE THROUGH PIPES.

Oil rigs like this one are used to get oil and natural gas from under the sea. A hole is drilled under the sea and into the ground to where the oil and gas are.

Fracking uses drills that go straight down into the ground and then straight across. Water, sand and chemicals are pumped into the holes. This breaks up the rock, letting out tiny pockets of gas and oil.

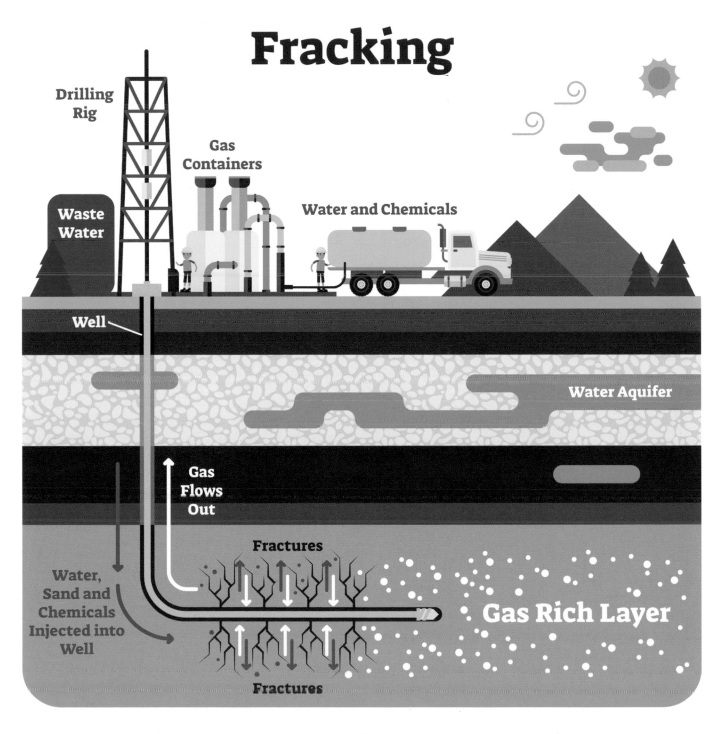

Fracking

Drilling Rig

Gas Containers

Water and Chemicals

Waste Water

Well

Water Aquifer

Gas Flows Out

Water, Sand and Chemicals Injected into Well

Fractures

Gas Rich Layer

Fractures

Coal is mined from the ground. If the coal is near the surface of the Earth, large **craters** are dug to reach the coal. If the coal is deeper in the Earth, long tunnels run underground to get to the coal.

UNDERGROUND COAL MINE

POLLUTED WATER AT A COAL MINE

Finding fossil fuels also does a lot of damage to the air we breathe, the water we drink and the land we live on. These mining methods also help cause global warming.

FINISHING THE FOSSIL FUELS

Fossil fuels are being used much quicker than they can be made, and we are using more of them every year. It takes hundreds of years to form fossil fuels. It won't be long until we run out.

It is estimated that if we keep using fossil fuels at the rate we are now, most of them will run out in the next 50–100 years.

Daily News

August, 2128

COAL'D ON A MINUTE!
THE FOSSIL FUELS ARE GONE

By J. Pointer

Today, after only 300 years of using fossil fuels, they have finally run out for good. We have taken all we can from the Earth and given nothing back. Scientists are quickly trying to put all of their focus into renewable energy sources. Funding is now being quickly put into solar, wind and hydro energy projects as scientists furiously try to keep up with the current demand for energy. All we can do for now is switch off the lights, turn off the television and look into making our own power. The world simply doesn't know how to survive without fossil fuels.

WHERE WILL WE GET OUR ENERGY WHEN FOSSIL FUELS RUN OUT?

ALTERNATIVE ENERGY

SOLAR PANELS, WIND TURBINES AND WATER POWER ARE TYPES OF RENEWABLE ENERGY.

Some of the world's most powerful wind turbines have blades that are bigger than the London Eye. The blades are so powerful that just one spin could power a UK home for a whole day!

SOLAR PANELS

Renewable energy uses processes that naturally occur and use them to create energy. This means it can't run out. Power from wind, waves and sunlight can be captured by machines and changed into power and heat.

HOW WE CAN HELP

DON'T BUY PLASTICS

Plastics contain by-products of fossil fuels. Instead of buying a new plastic item every time, get a reusable one, like this metal bottle.

WALK THE WALK

Lots of fossil fuels come from vehicles, so if you can walk, do! Every time you walk instead of using the car, you're saving the planet a tiny bit.

STOP TUMBLING

When you help your parents with the washing, use a washing line to hang up the wet clothes instead of tumble-drying them. Tumble dryers use lots of energy.

SPEEDY SHOWERS

It takes a lot of energy to heat up water. Even spending one minute less in the shower each time can save a lot of fossil fuels.

GLOSSARY

atmosphere	the mixture of gases that make up the air and surround the Earth
by-products	something that is produced by accident when making something else
craters	large shallow holes on the surface of something
decomposed	decay or rot
environment	the natural world
evaporated	turned from a liquid into a gas or vapour, usually through heat
global warming	the slow rise of the Earth's temperature
polluted	made harmful or dirty through the actions of humans
pressure	a physical force exerted on an object, which is caused by something pressing against it
sediment	small pieces of a solid material, for example sand, that can form a layer of rock over time

INDEX

Photocredits – Images are courtesy of Shutterstock.com. With thanks to Getty Images, Thinkstock Photo and iStockphoto.
Cover – Dagmara_K, N Azlin Sha, 1 – Geo-grafika, 2 – Denys Dolnikov, 3 – OSSYFFER, 4 – Crystal Eye Studio, 5 – Kodda, 6 – George W. Bailey, 7 – alfocome, Kostov, 8 – Maria Sbytova, 9 – Tony Baggett, 10 – Hung Chung Chih, 11 – Designua, 12 – Wittybear, 13 – Christopher Halloran, 14 – Lukasz Z, 15 – VectorMine, 16 – Mark Agnor, 17 – inacio pires, 18 – BlurryMe, 19 – Castleski, chrisw1964, 20 – Mimadeo, 21 – Hof, 22 – studioloco, Joyce Vincent, 23 – Africa Studio, MidoSemsen.